LITTLE NOTES

E. L KNIGHT

BookLeaf Publishing

India | USA | UK

Little Notes © 2021 E. L Knight

All rights reserved.

No part of this publication may be reproduced,
stored in a retrieval system, or transmitted, in
any form or by any means, electronic,
mechanical, photocopying, recording or
otherwise, without the prior written permission
of the presenters.

E. L Knight asserts the moral right to be
identified as author of this work.

Presentation by *BookLeaf Publishing*

Web: www.bookleafpub.com

E-mail: info@bookleafpub.com

ISBN : 9789358361728

First edition 2021

For My Divine Lights

All The World

PREFACE

For Twin Flames, Lightworkers, Spiritual Awakenings and Souls getting to know themselves on a deeper level.

These pages are for the rainy days, the warm summer sunsets, the tears in the eyes days, the heart beating love through the smile days, and for all those special, joy filled, dark, beautiful, challenging, perfectly imperfect moments in between that makes this life worthwhile and memorable.

DREAMING OF YOU

I have been dreaming of you
Each time I close my eyes there you are
You are the whisper in my heart
That I hear without words

You are in the songs that find me
Singing straight to my Soul
The sparkle in your eyes resides
In the corners of my blushing smile

Your voice resonates within me
In ways I cannot explain with words
There is a fire inside ignited
With passion desire and truth

I have been dreaming of you
For as long as I can remember
And as it is with all things

That cannot be explained
When all that can be left to do

After logic defies you

A great surrendering

To the depth of this love
In all ways that could be confined at this
dimension
An unconditional unbreakable bond

Tethered through space
Bending and stretching but never to part

Gathering star dust within movements
Evolving to the highest energetic degree
Retrieving Soul fragments left behind
From past lives and love shared

Only to find each other again and again
In this lifetime and eternity hereafter
There will never be another us
For you are me and I am you

And whenever I close my eyes
I am dreaming of you and I
And there in that Infinite space
We are home.

2

TIC TOC

Here I am

Tic Toc

Strong and robust or wistful and weakening

Tic Toc

Do you notice me

You can not see me

You can not feel me

I go by nonetheless

Tic Toc

How do you hold a conceptualized measurement
Do you hold me close to you or do you push me
away
Do you find me in the changing of the seasons
in the trees, in the skies
Or do you see me in the mirror and on the faces
of the ones you love

Do I bring you to your knees when I am stolen
Do I slow down the pace of your heart when
you are in the arms of the one you love
Do you miss me when I am gone

Do you appreciate me when I am here
Do I go by too fast when you lose yourself in
the things that bring you joy
Do I move too slowly when it feels like your
heart is breaking
In the Infinite space of the Cosmos, am I even
real

Do I exist or do I survive only in your mind, in
this material world to serve as a marker of a
past, present and future that is inconceivably
uncertain

Do you find me in the artwork of your life
Are you using me the way you need to
Love me while you have me

Here I am

Tic Toc.

3

CYCLES

Planting and growing

Seeding and sowing

Digging and weeding

Fasting and slowing

Shedding and peeling
Numbing and feeling

Cracking and breaking
Reeling and faking
Circling and learning
Longing and yearning

Healing and brightening

Darkening and lightening

Hellos and goodbyes
Emotions in eyes
Lessons and testings

Movements and restings
Constantly waiting

Loving and hating

Levels and dimensions
Manifesting intentions
Versions keep dying
Relentlessly trying
Reaching and stilling

Lowing and highing
Life keeps on drumming
Becoming unbecoming

Evolving the Soul
For its righteous Homecoming.

4

HOLD ON

I know you are holding on my darling
I need you to stay strong
I know you are feeling lost and lonely
And the days and nights feel long

Did you know that when you cry my dear
The skies they turn to grey
The rain comes pouring down like sheets
To wash your pain away

I know you feel alone my love
Please trust that it won't last
Once you break the chains that bind you
Love can pour in fast

From sources you will not expect
Can't see them through your tears
Even though they have been around you
For all times through the years

You must shift your frequency
The only way out is through
Trust the process don't doubt yourself
Light and dark are valid too

Feel your feelings true heart
And then release them when you're done
It's the only way to move on and up
And meet the rainbows and the sun

I know it is hard to feel this way
When you are down and feeling low
But please believe me when I say this
And heed this before you go

If no-one has told you this today
I am so proud of you dear Soul
Fighting battles silently
When you fall into that hole

I see you every time
I hear you all the thoughts you think
Search for me inside your heart
I am right there on the brink

I do not use words or thoughts
I am quieter than your mind
I am that warm feeling in your chest
The type of love that is kind

Find me all around you
Wherever that may be

I'm there on small faces and in hugs
Gratitude and laughter that's me

If you lose your way my darling
Remember it will pass
And when you want to feel my love
Connect inside and ask

You are beautiful the way you are
Perfectly flawed and whole
One day you will be home again
But for now expand your Soul

I love you so much you know
You are seen and heard and loved
Stop looking outside yourself for answers
I am inside you not above

Find me there
With Love.

5

LIGHTS

I like to sing, I like to dance
My heart leaps always at the chance
I toss my hair and flick my hand
I kick my legs and fly and land
I spin and turn, I lose myself
And find my Soul, my greatest wealth
When those big bright lights come on
And starts the beating of my song
I close my eyes and breathe in deep
My favorite feeling before I leap.

6

BREAKTHROUGH

Spinning and weaving
Weaving and spinning
Is it the end or
Is it the beginning
All the time spent
Alone on the ground
Walking slowly to somewhere

Trying not to be found
Curling and shrinking
At strange passers by
Dreaming that someday
Perhaps I would fly
Low living crawling
Just scraping along
Feeling like somehow
I didn't belong...

There has to be more
I can feel it inside
Just feeling so tired

I've struggled and tried

A nice little home
I have built for myself
And now for a nap
Up here on my shelf

Wait, what is happening
I am being pushed out
Put out of my comfy
Filling with doubt
My body is aching

I am getting a fright

My center is shaking

I am not feeling alright

Something is changing

It is opening up
What is this slime
I am covered in muck
Why am I hurting

So bad that it stings

What is this now, beside me
When did I grow wings

Uncurling this beauty

Shining brightly with light

It was all preparation

I am about to take flight
Up into the air
All colours and glow

I knew I was meant for this
I just needed to grow

NOW I can see...

That nothing was wrong
I was always heading towards
Where I truly belong.

DOOR WAYS

Doors can be many things
They can be exits or entrances

You can be coming or going
You can open them and shut them
You can swing them or slam them
Doors can be locked and bolted
Doors can be unlocked and transparent
They can be decorated and fun
They can be old worn and scary
You can stand in between them
You can run there for safety
Doors can be for watching

Doors can be for leaving or returning

Doors can be sanded repainted, remade
Doors can be punched kicked and broken

You can walk past them without noticing

You can have to lock them three times

You might love them if they are slightly unique

You might feel a need to always adjust them

Doors can welcome ones you love
Doors can keep out ones you don't

Some have secrets and passwords
Some work with only the right keys
Some have a simple working handle
Some are built with riches
Doors can feel easy to open
Doors can feel completely impossible

Doors can be material
Doors can be metaphorical
Doors to open
Doors to close
Doors to run to
Doors to walk away from
Doors for all
Doors to choose
Door Ways.

8

UNITE

How old were you

When you realized your worth
When you discovered in fact
You belonged to the Earth
What day was it
When you first found out
You were conditioned with lies
Fed fear and Self doubt
What did it take
To stand up and say No
No more of these atrocities
No more watching this show

Which historical event
Made it so clear to see
You have been living in darkness
A hoax that you are free

What age did you stop
Believing all that you hear
And start searching for truth
Behind programs and fear

When did you know

Beyond reasonable doubt
You can fight for your rights

Get off this paved route
Which was the moment
You could no longer ignore
The countless lives lost

Economic blood on the floor

Which of the narratives
Did you hear as the truth
Pushed concerns to the side

Sworn nail and tooth
When was the year

You stood up for your own

You began digging deeper

Way past what you were shown
How did you feel

On the day that you learned

You had every right

To feel more than concerned

How did you respond

When you turned on the light

When you realized Freedom
Was everyone's birthright

Did you take to the socials

Did you tell all your friends

Did you suddenly know

An era had come to its ends

Have you found all the others

They are waking up too

Did you know there are more

Lightworkers like you

A New Earth is waiting

Being born from your mind

Sustainable free energy

Creation loving and kind

Abundance for all

Right here from the Earth

Lightworkers are calling

For your spiritual rebirth

Holding the grid
Waiting for your ascension

You must leave behind

Any fear and apprehension

Step into your own
Let your heart break wide open

You are constantly guided

Being shown and awoken
Will today be the day
You start asking how
You are leveling up

Your time is Now.

9

EARTH

Hovering sparkling emanating light
Out of the atmosphere diamond bright
Lingering warmth glowing golden entice
Depth in the shadows below frozen ice
Outstretched indigo blanketing dreams
Nautical sprouting blooming in streams
Technical launches pervading connection
Oppression depression dividing in section
Holistic intrinsic Spirit tapestry weaving
Over desolate sands fire rings heaving
Planetary ascension Consciousness birth
Evolution restitution Love inheriting Earth.

DIVINITY

Mirror in the eyes
Synchronicity in the sound
Intertwining magic light

Infinite space unwound
Cosmic dance dimensions

Stoic strength unfold
Softness in resistance

Flow anahata notes untold
Ancient akashic lives
Magnetic elements alive

Merging fields of light
Energetic sparking thrive

Tantric Divine alignment

Sacred Flames Soul two
Unbound everlasting love

Complete with Violet hue.

ONE

Lost in the stars
Transcending our skin
Dancing in twilight
Essence within
Igniting beginning
Surrender and flow

Closer we get
Higher we go
Mind into mind
Heart into heart
Joining in timelines
Never to part
Love joyful innocence

Playfulness laughter
Find us in this and each
Lifetime hereafter.

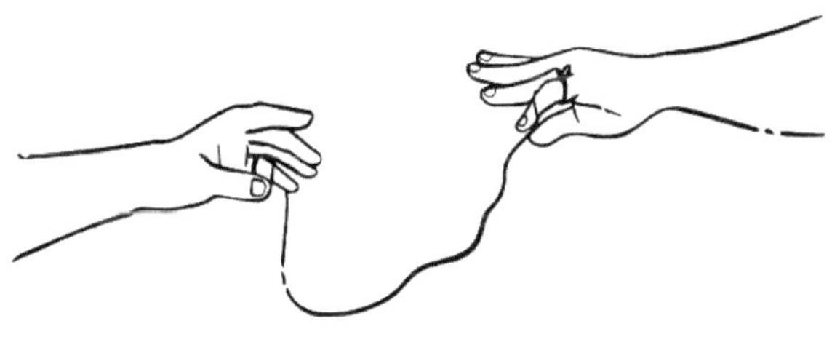

12

SOMEDAY

The temple of heart can leave one in dark

Not knowing when to return

Days turn to weeks turn to months in the silence

Leaving the flame on to burn
Quarrel the heart and the mind 'til they suffer

Finding somewhere to save space

Deep down below under yearning and longing

Creating this heavenly place
Battle the reach windows averting

Knowing is pushed to the way
Turn to look back with a compass on track
Waiting for somewhere

Someday.

13

LITTLE ONE

Crinkled tiny little toes

Warm soft scrunched up feet
Delicate little hands and nose
Meeting heartbeat to heartbeat
Beautiful blinking big bright eyes
A yawn big stretch and curled
A Soul born new but old and wise
Bringing light into the world
Clasped around an awestruck finger

A small hand squeezes tight
A love like this to last and linger
And deepen day and night
Head to head and nose to nose

Giggles laughter tears and cuddles

Soft forehead kisses loving flows
Midnight plays and wet milk puddles
Eyes that stare into the heart
Learning together as we roam
Knowing right from the very start
Wherever we go we are home
Crawling learning walking now
Clapping soothing as you grow
Holding jumping talking now

Teaching me more as we go
Taller taller making friends

No matter what the day be
This love my darling never ends
You will always be my baby.

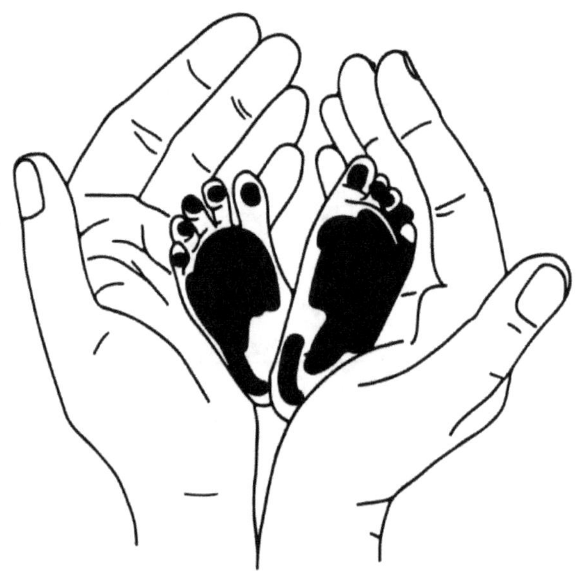

14

YOU KNOW

The answer was found
Not on the streets

Not empty space rooms
Or entangled in sheets

Not up in the skies
On socials or text

It wasn't in replays
Not past dreams or next
It wasn't in others

Not carried in cash
It couldn't be traced

Or found with a #hash
It didn't use words
From the chest it did flow
Saying deep in your heart

You already know.

15
Healing Roots

Strong roots grow outwards from the feet

Deep down into the ground
Spreading right into the core of Earth
Red warm glow deep exhale sound
Knowing there is comfort here

Set on a safe foundation

Mindfully bringing forth the inner child

With a soft and loving invitation

Holding lovingly gently in the space

Affirming aloud you are here with me

Releasing all the lessons prior to this

That now no longer need to be
Letting go of the past fear and doubt
Instability can now be ceased
Integrating energies into the being

Allowing past wounds to be released
Connected here with Mother Earth

Feeling protected safe and loved

Bringing hands up to the vortex sky
Opening to gifts from up above

Golden light pours through the body

Spills out returning to the Earth
Cleansing purifying all energy centers
Mind Body Spirit set for rebirth.

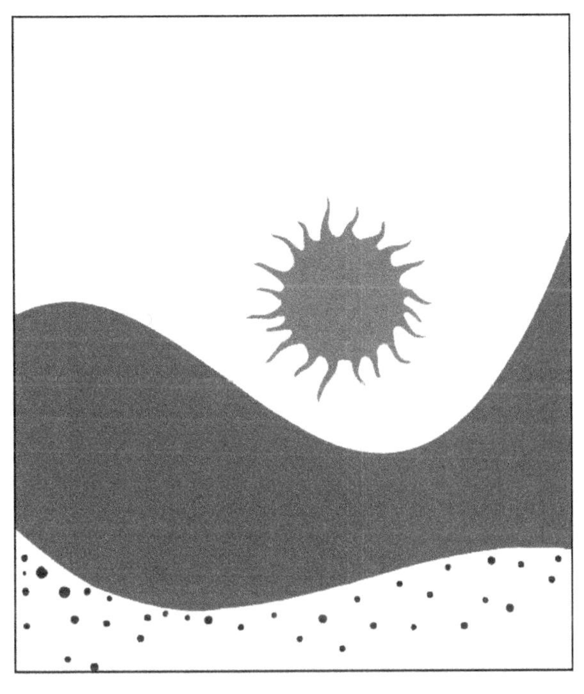

16
GROWING UP

When I grew up they told me I could be

A career from the choices here you see

What is it what is it that you want to be

A tradesman a carer professional degree

Choose a direction and then once you know

Into the full-time workplace you go

I did not want to be one how could I choose

I was tired of searching and asking for clues

I wanted to do everything I had said very young

Well sorry my dear that just can't be done

You can not do it all so don't even try

I have spent my entire life wondering why

I did not want to choose one path with locks

I was not made to fit inside of a box

I can not be just one I had yelled very loud

I will not swim upstream and follow the crowd

I did not come here to work to survive

I came here to be Human to feel truly alive

I came here to dance to sing and to love

I came to connect with my heart from above

I did not like the sales I did not need the pitch

Did not want to spend time solving algorithms
glitch
I just wanted to play and enjoy what I do

I knew that I could I knew that to be true
One synchronized day I met an old Soul

Who spoke of alchemy life's true gold

I was told that to thrive at our God given best

Tune into the power we can access and manifest
Create with your heart and build your reality

Stop playing so small bound with 9 - 5 gravity

Start from within and connect to your Source

Follow your intuition with inspired action of course

It was then I remembered my truest Divinity

Whatever I do is with love and sovereignty

What matters much more than one job or career

Is the impact I make with this precious time here

Living in flow with integrity and reverence

Connecting to God with affinity and resonance

Imagine when we can authentically relate

Connect with natural skill sets that make us feel great

Learn to invest our energy and time

To open our gifts and help others to shine

Humans have the power of alchemy you know

Our minds unlock more and more as we grow

Do not ever settle for less than you are

It is time to transform and raise a new bar

Ascend from the old paradigm existential

It is time to transcend and embrace your
potential.

17

THE OTHER SIDE

The stars keep shining in the sky
The breeze it still blows warm
I miss you when I am by myself
And when the skies begin to storm
An empty space where you used to be
Takes hold inside my heart
I miss you every day and night

Wishing we had not had to part
We did not need words you and I
Your eyes your touch your nose

I miss the days you sat with me
How fast the time it goes
I had you until you grew so old

Your hair had turned to grey
I could not ask for more than that

I loved you every single day
I will remember you forever

And I know it is not the end
See you when our Souls are free

My best and special friend.

www.ingramcontent.com/pod-product-compliance
Lightning Source LLC
LaVergne TN
LVHW051231200726

843510LV00011B/1551